GECKO^s

MORE
BEAD ANIMALS

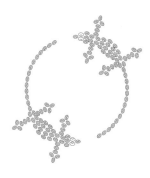

Drew Wilkens

Bead Man

Press

Issaquah, Washington

ISBN 0-9663591-1-9

All illustrations by Drew Wilkens

Printed in the USA

First printing November, 1998

Contents

Introduction

My first book, <u>Geckos & Other Bead Animals</u> was a tremendous success. Children all across the United States and Canada have embraced the craft. Volume II is not just more of the same, but reflects new techniques that others have shared with me along the way.

Bead Animals are a fun and imaginative activity. You can hang them from your backpacks or trade them with your friends. Bead Animals are a great craft fund raiser and beading can help develop fine motor skills.

I want to thank everyone for their letters and email. I enjoy hearing from you and about the positive experiences and success that you have had with the book.

Have a great time with this book and keep art in your life.

- Drew Wilkens
"The Bead Man"

Getting Started
Beads

If you are just learning, it is a good idea to start out with large "Pony" beads. Pony beads are 9mm in diameter and have a large hole. They can be made of glass or plastic. Plastic beads are affordable, light weight and are easily found in bead or craft stores. As your skills develop, try smaller beads like 6mm, No. 6 seed beads or tiny seed beads like 10 or 11.

 9mm

 6mm

◉ No.6

◎ No.10

String

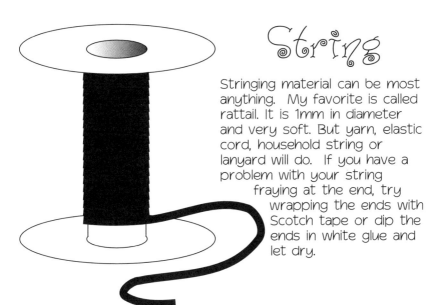

Stringing material can be most anything. My favorite is called rattail. It is 1mm in diameter and very soft. But yarn, elastic cord, household string or lanyard will do. If you have a problem with your string fraying at the end, try wrapping the ends with Scotch tape or dip the ends in white glue and let dry.

Key Ring

Geckos are a backpack must! Add a key ring and you are on your way.

Basic Stitch - Body

There are several types of stitches used in this book. Most of the projects require the most basic called the body stitch..

STEP 1

String the number of beads necessary for the first row of your design Fold the string in half, and let the beads slide to the middle.

STEP 2

Place beads for the next row on side **B** of the string The side you start with does not affect the design.

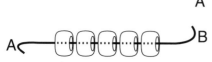

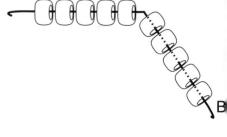

STEP 3

Thread side **A** of your string through the beads on side **B** going the opposite way.

STEP 4

Pull tight.

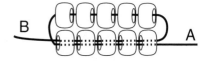

STEP 5

Repeat steps 2, 3 and 4 for each row. That is all there is to it!

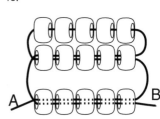

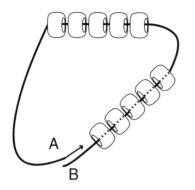

Basic Stitch - Leg

There is variation in the leg stitch, usually the number of toes. The following example is from the three toed gecko.

STEP 1

Place 6 beads on your string (3 beads for the leg, 3 beads for the toe).

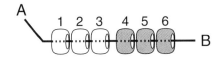

STEP 2

Skipping beads #4-5-6 and thread side **B** back through beads #3-2-1 and pull tight.

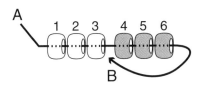

The leg may be too far from the body. To move it closer, grab the center toe bead (#5) and pull side **B**. This will slide the leg closer to the body.

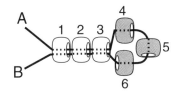

Basic Stitch - Ear

STEP 1

To create the ear, place 8 beads on side **B**, of your string.

STEP 2

Bring the string back through the beads by skipping bead #8 and threading through, in order, #6 then #7. Pull tight.

STEP 3

Thread through beads #4, then #5. Pull tight.

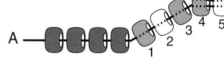

STEP 4

Thread through beads #2, then #3. Pull tight.

STEP 5

Thread through beads #1. Pull tight and continue the pattern using the body stitch and leg stitch.

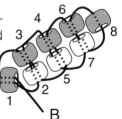

Review:
Threading order
1 - 2 - 3 - 4 - 5 -
6 - 7 - 8 - 6 - 7 -
4 - 5 - 2 - 3 - 1

Basic Stitch - Tail

Although the tail is made with a simple 1 bead body stitch, it is often a point of confusion.

STEP 1

When you reach the tail, place 1 bead on side **B** of the string.

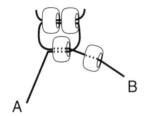

STEP 2

Thread string **A** the opposing direction

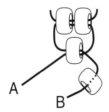

STEP 3

Pull tight and repeat.

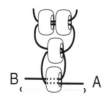

Flag

STEP 1

Body Stitch: String 6 beads for the first row. (3 blue, red, white, red). Fold the string in half and let the beads slide to the middle

A   B

STEP 2

Place 6 beads from row 2 on side **B** of your string. (red, white, red, 3 blue)

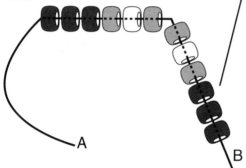

A

B

STEP 3

Thread side **A** of your string through the beads on side **B** going the opposite way.

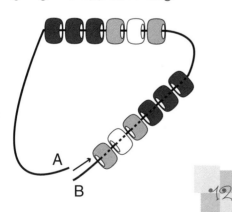

A

B

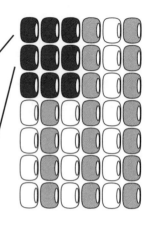

Factoid:

The first flag of the United States was adopted on July 4, 1~~777~~ and had 13 stripes and 13 stars. One star for each of the original 13 colonies. Today's flag has the same 13 stripes, but a star count of 50. One star for each state.

Body stitch

❖ Colors ❖

	Navy Blue	(9)
	Red	(18)
	White	(15)
	String	3 ft.

12

STEP 4

Pull both ends tight

STEP 5

Following the pattern, create each row by repeating steps 2, 3 and 4.

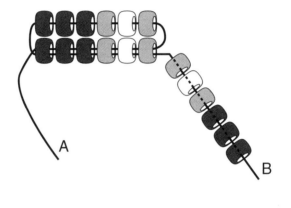

STEP 6

When complete, tie off each end. For extra security place a small dot of glue on the knots.

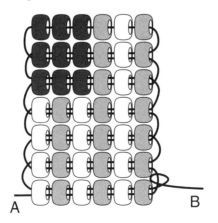

Pencil

STEP 1
Body Stitch: Place 1 black bead on your string. Fold the string in half and let the bead slide to the middle

STEP 2
Place 2 beads from row 2 on side **B** of your string.

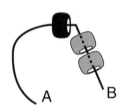

STEP 3
Thread side **A** of your string through the beads on side **B** going the opposite way.

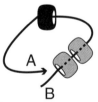

STEP 4
Pull tight. Continue the pattern using steps 2 & 3. (The next row uses 3 beads.)

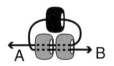

Factoid:
The lead pencil contains no lead. The pencil is made by mixing graphite, clay and water into a paste and molding it into rods. The rods are baked and inserted into wood holders.

Body stitch

▪ Colors ▪	
⬛ Black	(1)
🟧 Orange	(12)
⬜ Gray	(8)
🟫 Tan	(9)
⬜ Yellow	(24)
▬ String	3 ft.

Bracelet

STEP 1

Start by placing 1 bead on the center of your string. Match the two ends together and let the bead fall to the middle.

STEP 2

Place 1 bead on side **A** and 1 bead on side **B**.

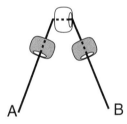

STEP 3

Place 1 bead on side **B** of your string and thread side **A** through the bead in the opposite direction.

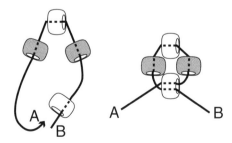

STEP 4

Repeat steps 2 & 3 until you reach the desired length. Tie a knot at the end. Elastic cord works well for this project.

:: Colors ::	
Green	(18)
Yellow	(24)
String	2 ft.

15

Corn

STEP 1

Body Stitch: Place 1 bead on your string. Match the ends together and let the bead slide to the middle

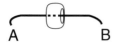

STEP 2

Following the pattern, place 2 beads on side **B** of your string.

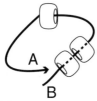

STEP 3

Thread side **A** of your string through both beads in the opposite direction. Pull tight.

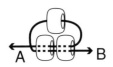

Repeat steps 2 & 3 using three beads.

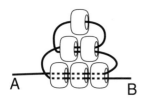

Factoid:

Corn, introduced to the world by the natives of North America, not only tastes great but is used to make flour, syrup, whiskey, cooking oil and as a gasoline additive.

Body stitch, Leg stitch

▦ **Colors** ▦

◖	Green	(18)
◖	Yellow	(24)
▬	String	3 ft.

STEP 4

Continue following the pattern using the "body stitch" until you reach the leaves of the corn.

STEP 5

To make the leaf of the corn, place 4 beads on the B side of your string

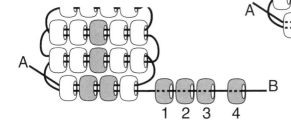

1 2 3 4

STEP 6

Skipping bead #4, thread side B of your string through beads #3, #2 then #1 and pull tight. To move the leaf close to the corn body, hold bead #4 with two fingers and pull string

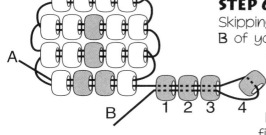

1 2 3 4

STEP 7

Make the other leaf on side A using steps 5 & 6. Then place 1 bead on side A, and 1 bead on side B.

Finish the pattern using the body stitch shown in steps 2 & 3,

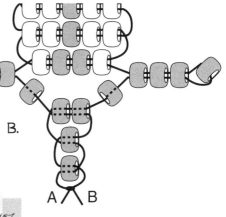

B.

A ⋀ B

Cross

STEP 1

Body Stitch: Using the body stitch as illustrated in page 6, build 3 rows of 3 beads each.

A   B

STEP 2

To make the arms of the cross, place 6 beads on side **B** of the string,

A

B

1 2 3 4 5 6

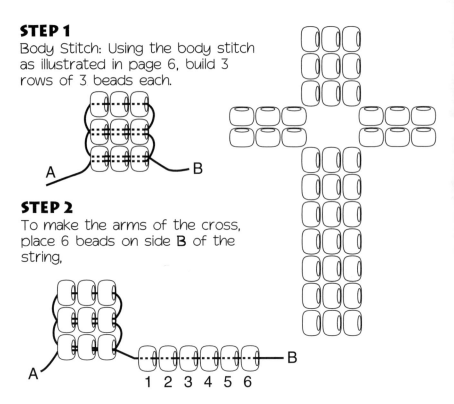

STEP 3

Skipping beads #6-5, thread side **B** of your string back through bead #3 then bead #4 and pull tight.

Move the beads closer to the cross by holding beads #5 and #6 with two fingers and pulling on side **B**.

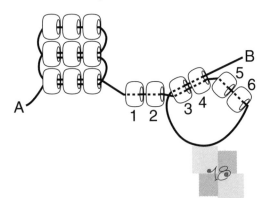

A

B

1 2 3 4 5 6

Body stitch, Ear stitch

⠿ **Colors** ⠿	
⬜ White	(42)
⬛ String	3 ft.

18

STEP 4
Thread side **B** through bead #1 then bead #2.

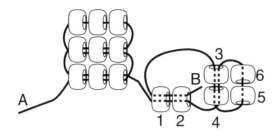

STEP 5
Pull tight. You may need to help the beads straighten out into a line.

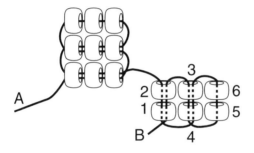

STEP 6
Make the left arm of the cross by repeating steps 3, 4 and 5 using side **A** of the string, Continue using the "body stitch" to finish the pattern. Tie each end.

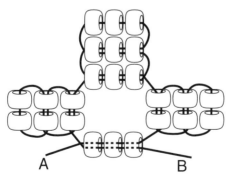

Bull Head

STEP 1

We need to make the bull head upside down. Start with the nose. Place 4 beads on your string. Match the ends of the string and let the bead fall to the center.

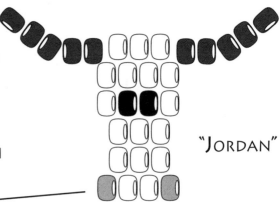

"JORDAN"

A — B

STEP 2

Following the pattern, place three beads on side **B** of your string.

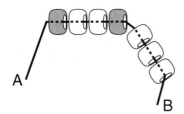

A

B

Factoid:

The bull is a symbol of strength. When the stock market is strong it is said to be a "bull market" What professional basketball organization uses this symbol for their team? (Chicago Bulls)

STEP 3

Thread side **A** of your string through all beads on side **B**. Pull tight.

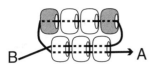

B → A

Body stitch,
Leg stitch

▦ Colors ▦	
Black	(2)
Brown	(10)
Pink	(2)
White	(17)
String	3 ft.

STEP 4

Continue the pattern using steps 2 & 3 until you reach the horns.

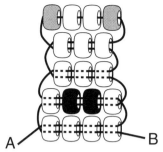

STEP 5

To make the horns, place 5 beads on side **B** of your string.

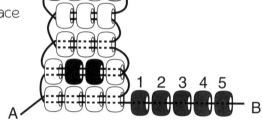

STEP 6

Skipping bead #5, thread side **B** through bead #4, skip #3 and thread through beads #2-1. Repeat steps 5 and 6 on side **A**.

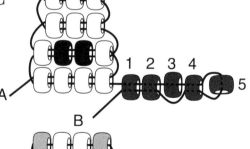

STEP 7

Finish with one last row using the body stitch. Tie each end at the head.

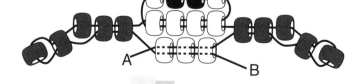

Reindeer Head

STEP 1

We need to make the reindeer head upside down. Start with the nose. Place 1 bead on your string. Match the ends and let the bead fall to the center.

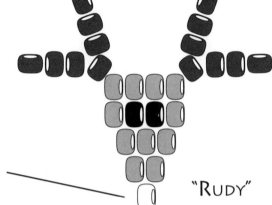

"RUDY"

A————◻————B

STEP 2

Following the pattern, place two beads on side **B** of your string.

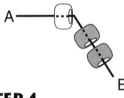

STEP 3

Thread side **A** of your string through both beads on side **B**. Pull tight.

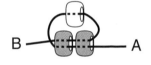

STEP 4

Continue the pattern using steps 2 & 3 until you reach the antlers.

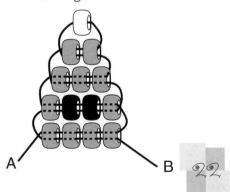

Body stitch, Leg stitch

▦ Colors ▦	
⬛ Black	(2)
🟤 Brown	(14)
🟡 Tan	(11)
⬜ Red	(1)
▬ String	3 ft.

STEP 5

To make the antlers, place 4 beads on side **B** of your string.

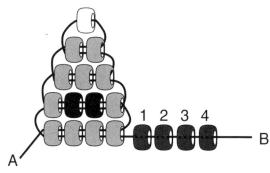

STEP 6

Skipping bead #4, thread side **B** back through beads #3-2.

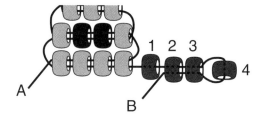

STEP 7

Place 3 more beads on side **B** of your string.

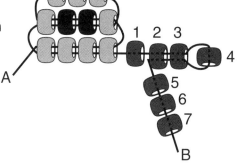

STEP 8

Skipping bead #7, thread side **B** back through beads #6-5 then #1 and pull tight. Thread back through a bead on the reindeer head and tie. Repeat steps 5 thru 8 on side **A** of your string.

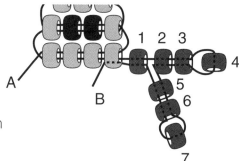

Golf Counter

STEP 1
Fold your string in half to determine the middle. Make a knot creating a 2 inch loop at the top

STEP 2
Place 1 bead on side **B** of your string.

STEP 3
Thread side **A** of your string through the bead in the opposite direction. Pull Tight.

"Elastic cord works best"

STEP 4
Continue with the pattern by repeating steps 1 and 2. Before adding the last bead, allow 2 inches of space in your string and tie a knot. Add the last bead and knot again.

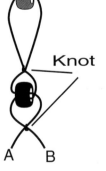

Knot

USING YOUR COUNTER
The top loop is used to secure your counter to your belt. To begin, move all of the beads to the top of the counter. After each stroke, move one bead down to the bottom.

Tail stitch

:: Colors ::	
Black	(1)
Blue	(5)
Yellow	(5)
▬ String	3 ft.

24

Gecko

STEP 1
Place the "nose" bead in the center of your string. Match the ends of your string together and let the bead fall to the middle.

STEP 2
Following the pattern from the top down, place two beads on side **B** of your string.

STEP 3
Take side **A** of your string and thread through the two bead in the opposite direction.

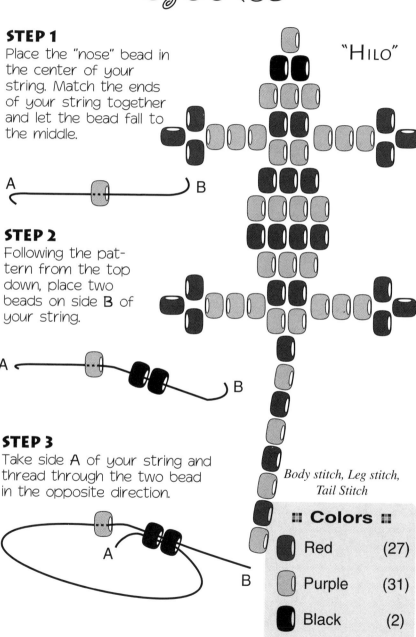

"HILO"

Body stitch, Leg stitch, Tail Stitch

⠿ Colors ⠿

⬤	Red	(27)
◯	Purple	(31)
⬤	Black	(2)
▬▬	String	4 ft.

STEP 4
Pull the two ends tight.

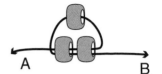

STEP 5
Refer to the layout for the next row. Place three beads on string **B**. Repeat steps 2, 3 and 4 (body stitch) until you reach the legs.

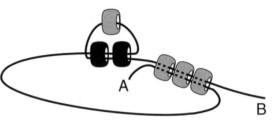

STEP 6
Leg stitch: To make the leg, place 6 beads on side **B**.

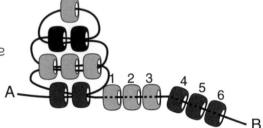

STEP 7
Skip beads #6,#5,#4 and come back through #3,#2 and #1. Pull tight. Repeat steps 6 & 7 to make the leg on side **A**.

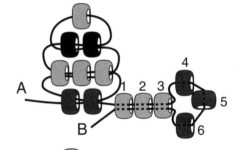

STEP 8
Continue the pattern until your reach the tail.

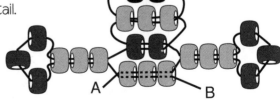

STEP 9

The tail is made using the body stitch. Place 1 bead on side **B** of your string. Thread side **A** in the opposite direction, pull tight.

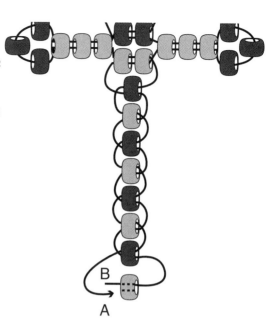

BUG EYE OPTION

STEP 1

To make the eyes bug out, place 1 "eye color" bead on side **A** of your string.

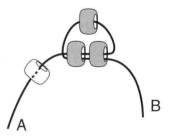

STEP 2

Thread side **A** back through the bead from the previous row and pull tight. Be sure to slide the beads close together. Repeat of side **B**. Continue the gecko from Step 5.

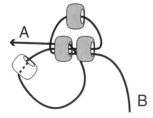
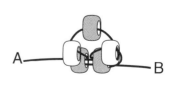

Gecko Baby

STEP 1

Place the "nose" bead on your string. Match the two ends of the string together and let the bead fall to the center

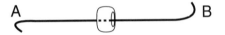

A   B

STEP 2

Following the pattern from the top down, place two "eye" beads on side **B** of your string.

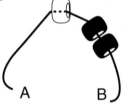

A   B

STEP 3

Thread side **A** of your string through both beads

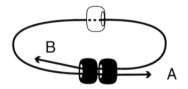

B

A

STEP 4

Pull the two ends tight.

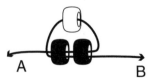

A   B

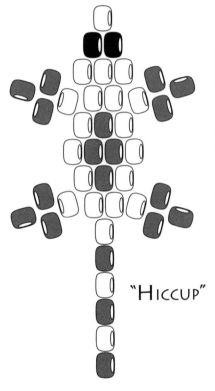

"HICCUP"

Body stitch, Leg stitch, Tail Stitch

▪ Colors ▪

⬛	Black	(2)
🟦	Blue	(19)
⬜	Pink	(21)
▬	String	3 ft.

28

STEP 5

Refer to the layout for the next row. Place three beads on string **B**. Repeating steps 3 & 4 continue until you reach the legs.

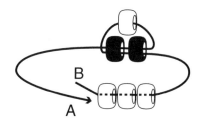

STEP 6

Leg Stitch: To make the leg, place 4 beads on side **B** of your string.

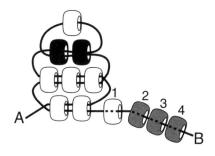

STEP 7

Skipping beads #4-3-2 and thread side **B** through bead #1 and pull tight. To make the leg move close to the body, hold bead #3 with two fingers and pull string **B**. Make the other leg using steps 6 & 7.

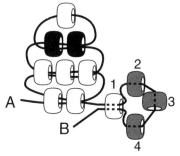

STEP 8

Continue following the pattern to create the body and legs of the gecko.

Tail Stitch: The tail is made by placing 1 bead on side **B** of your string and threading side **A** through in the opposite direction.

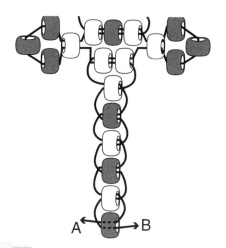

Centipede

"MAXIMILLION LEGS"

STEP 1

Place 3 beads on your string. Match the ends together and let the beads fall to the middle.

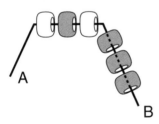

A —▭▭▭— B

STEP 2

Following the pattern, place 3 beads on side **B** of your string.

STEP 3

Thread side **A** of your string through the beads on side **B** going the opposite way.

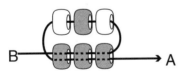

B ————→ A

Factoid:

A centipede has 30 or more legs. They are night hunters and catch their prey using paralyzing poisonous jaws. Some types can grow up to 11 inches long.

Body stitch

∷ **Colors** ∷	
▮ Dk. Blue	(12)
▯ Lt. Blue	(42)
▯ White	(2)
▬▬ String	4 ft.

30

STEP 4

Following the pattern, make another row of beads by placing 3 beads on side **B** and threading side **A** through them.

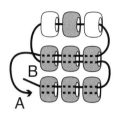

STEP 5

To make the little feet, place 1 bead on side **B** of your string..

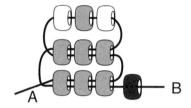

STEP 6

Thread side **B** of your string on the bead marked X and pull tight. Repeat steps 5 & 6 of side **A** of your string.

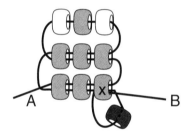

STEP 7

Continue the pattern using the steps above until you reach the end. Tie a knot and glue.

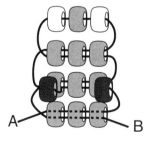

Star

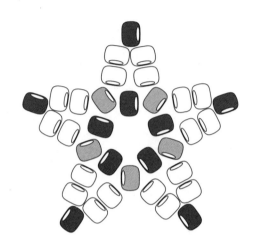

Factoid:

Some people believe that the first visible star of the evening is a wishing star. Be the first to see it and cast your wish. You never know what can happen.

What star can only be seen in the daytime? (the sun)

STEP 1

Place 10 beads on your string.

A   B

STEP 2

Tie the string in a knot so that the beads form a circle. Leave 6 inches of string on side A, leave side B long.

A   B

A
B

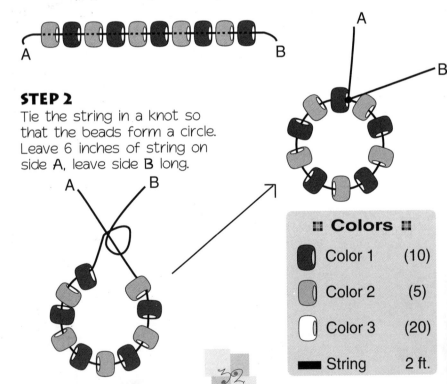

⚏ Colors ⚏	
⬤ Color 1	(10)
⬤ Color 2	(5)
⬤ Color 3	(20)
▬ String	2 ft.

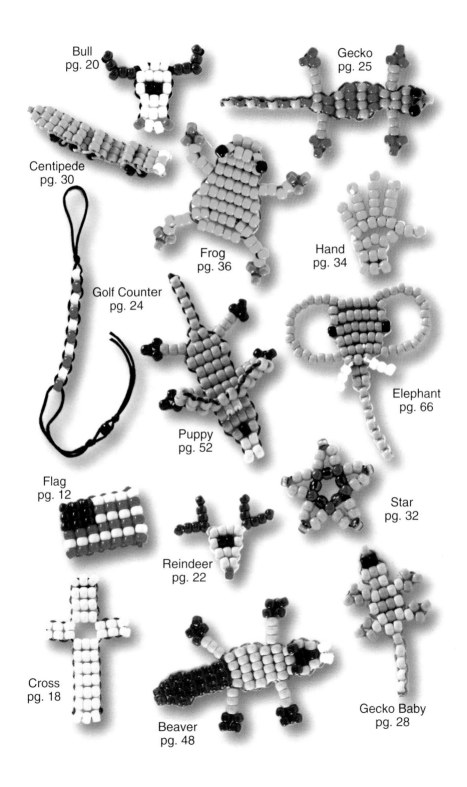

Bull
pg. 20

Gecko
pg. 25

Centipede
pg. 30

Golf Counter
pg. 24

Frog
pg. 36

Hand
pg. 34

Elephant
pg. 66

Puppy
pg. 52

Flag
pg. 12

Reindeer
pg. 22

Star
pg. 32

Cross
pg. 18

Beaver
pg. 48

Gecko Baby
pg. 28

STEP 3

Add 5 beads to side **B** of your string.

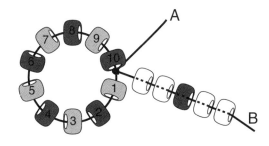

STEP 4

Thread the end of side **B** through the bead marked #2 and pull tight.

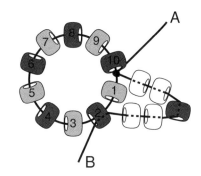

STEP 5

Repeat steps 3 & 4. Thread 5 beads on side **B**, and then through bead number #4. Pull tight.

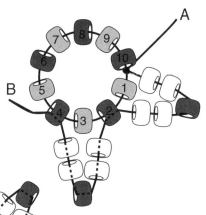

STEP 6

Repeat steps 3 & 4. Attaching the points of your star to beads #6, #8 and #10. Tie the ends of the string together in a knot.

Hand

STEP 1

Start the hand from the bottom using the "body stitch"

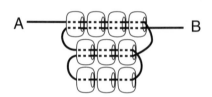

A —————— B

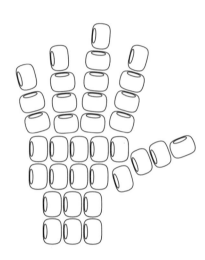

STEP 2

To make the thumb, place 4 beads on side **B** of your string.

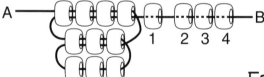

A —————— 1 2 3 4 —— B

Factoid:

There are 27 bones in the human hand. Each finger has 3 bones called phalanges.

STEP 3

Skipping bead #4, thread side **B** back through beads #3 and #2. Skip bead #1.

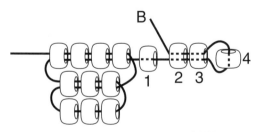

B
1 2 3 4

Body stitch
Leg stitch

:: Colors ::

⬜ Turquoise (35)

▬▬ String   4 ft.

STEP 4
Using the body stitch, make another row by placing 5 beads on side **B** and threading the opposite direction with side **A**.

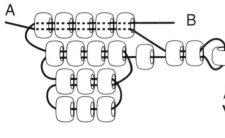

STEP 7
Skipping bead #4 thread side **B** back through beads #3-2-1, then through a bead in the hand.

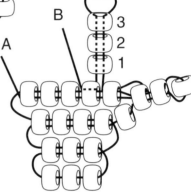

STEP 5
Thread side **B** of your string through the bead marked 1, then through bead marked 2

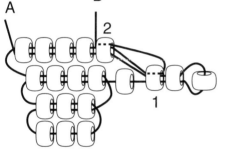

STEP 8
Create each finger using steps 6 & 7. Tie the ends of your string together.

STEP 6
Make the fingers by placing 4 beads on side **B**.

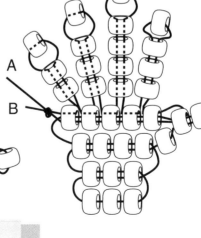

Frog

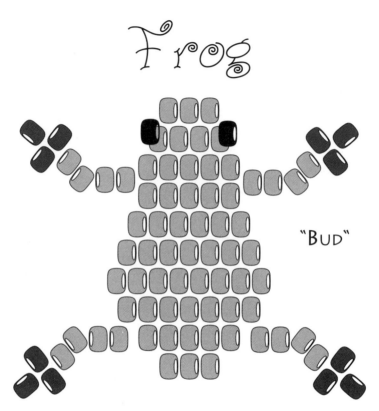

"BUD"

Factoid:

There is a frog that thinks he is a dog. The barking frog found in Texas makes a sound that is often mistaken for a barking dog.

STEP 1

Starting at the top of the pattern, place 3 (green) beads on your string. Match the two ends of the string together and let the beads fall in the middle.

A ——————————— B

Body stitch, Leg stitch,

▨ **Colors** ▨	
Dk. Green	(12)
Lt. Green	(69)
Black	(2)
▬ String	5 ft.

STEP 2

Place 4 (green) beads on side **B** of your string.

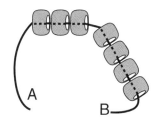

STEP 3

Thread side **A** of your string through the 4 (green) beads and pull tight.

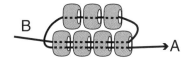

STEP 4

Add 1 (black) bead on side **B** and thread the end of your string through the last bead on the row. This will make the bug eyes.

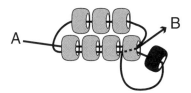

STEP 5

Repeat step 4 using side A of your string. Make another row using 5 (green) beads as shown in steps 2 & 3.

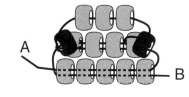

STEP 6

Leg Stitch: To make the leg, place 7 beads on side **B** of your string.

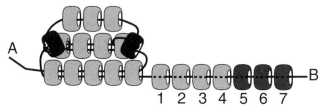

STEP 7

Skipping beads #7-6-5 thread side **B** back through #4, skip #3 and thread #2-1. Pull tight

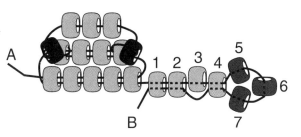

STEP 8

Repeat step 7 & 8 on side **A**. Continue pattern.

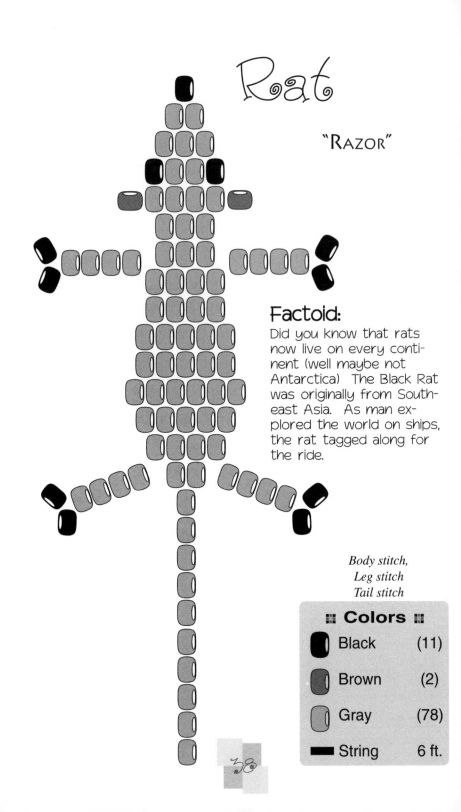

Rat

"RAZOR"

Factoid:

Did you know that rats now live on every continent (well maybe not Antarctica) The Black Rat was originally from Southeast Asia. As man explored the world on ships, the rat tagged along for the ride.

Body stitch,
Leg stitch
Tail stitch

▒ Colors ▒

▮	Black	(11)
▮	Brown	(2)
▯	Gray	(78)
▬	String	6 ft.

STEP 1

The rat is very much like the gecko. For detailed instructions look at the gecko on page 25. To make the rat follow the pattern and build the head using the body stitch.

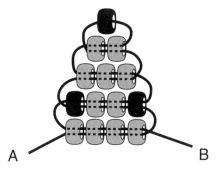

A   B

STEP 2

To make the 3-D ears, place 1 bead on side **B** of your string.

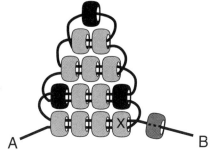

A   B

STEP 3

Thread side B through the bead marked X on the head of the rat. Pull tight. Repeat steps 2 & 3 on side **A**.

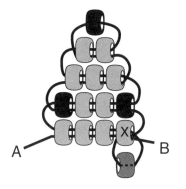

A   B

STEP 4

Continue the body stitch until you reach the leg.

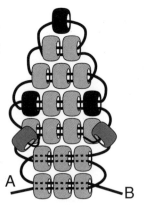

STEP 5

Leg Stitch: To make the leg, place 6 beads on side **B** of your string.

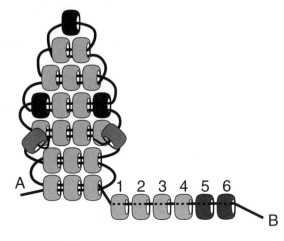

STEP 6

Skipping beads #6-5 thread side **B** back through #4,3,2,1. Pull tight

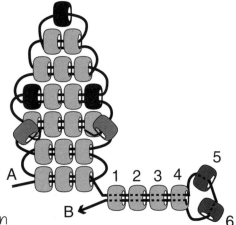

STEP 7

Repeat step 5 & 6 on side **A**. Continue pattern.

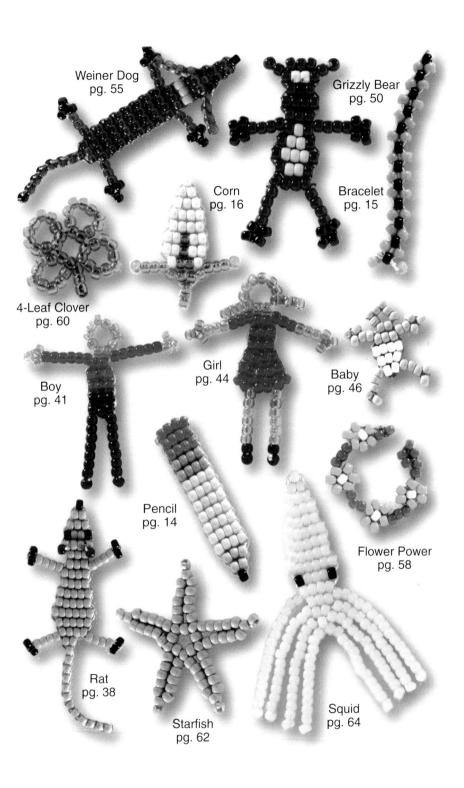

Weiner Dog
pg. 55

Grizzly Bear
pg. 50

Corn
pg. 16

Bracelet
pg. 15

4-Leaf Clover
pg. 60

Boy
pg. 41

Girl
pg. 44

Baby
pg. 46

Pencil
pg. 14

Flower Power
pg. 58

Rat
pg. 38

Starfish
pg. 62

Squid
pg. 64

Boy

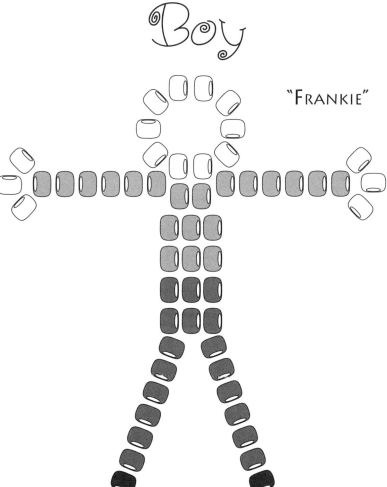

"FRANKIE"

*Body stitch,
Leg stitch*

STEP 1
Place 8 beads on the center of
your string.

A  B

:: **Colors** ::	
Brown	(4)
Blue	(18)
Red	(20)
Yellow	(16)
String	4 ft.

STEP 2
Place two beads A
on the B side
your string

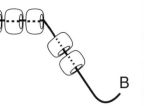

STEP 3
Take side A of your
string and thread the
two beads.

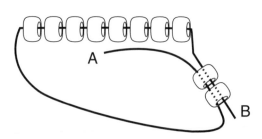

STEP 4
Pull the two ends
tight to form a circle

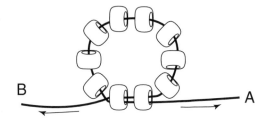

STEP 5
To make the arm, place 9 beads on side B of you string.

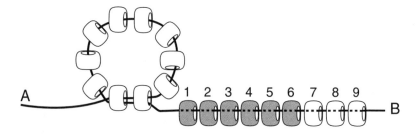

STEP 6

Skipping beads #9-8-7, thread side **B** back through beads #6-5-4-3-2-1. To make the arm move closer to the body, hold bead #8 with two fingers and pull the end of string side **B**.

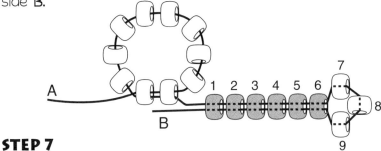

STEP 7

Repeat step 6 on side **A** of your string. Following the pattern, make the body of your bead person using the "body stitch" (page 6) until you reach the legs.

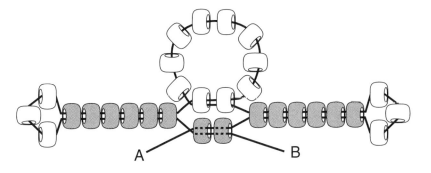

STEP 8

To make the leg, place 8 beads on side **B** of your string. Skipping bead #8, thread side **B** back through beads #7-6-5-4-3-2-1. Repeat on side A.

To finish, pass both ends through the body and tie.

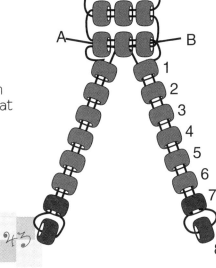

43

Girl

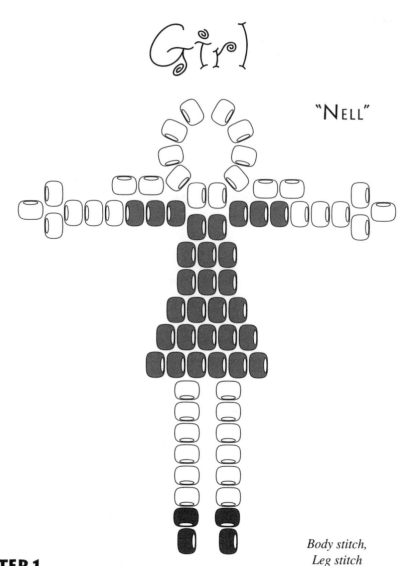

"Nell"

STEP 1

The girl is made very similar to the boy. Place 8 beads on the center of your string.

A ⌒───────────────⌒ B

*Body stitch,
Leg stitch*

▥ **Colors** ▥

▥ Brown	(4)
▥ Red	(29)
▥ Yellow	(38)
▬ String	5 ft.

44

STEP 2
Place two beads
on the B side of
your string

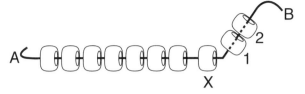

STEP 3
Skipping bead #2,
thread side **B**
through bead #1.

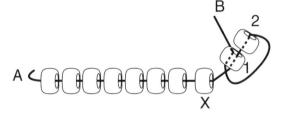

STEP 4
Thread side **B** through
bead marked X and
pull tight. You may
have to work the
beads to get them
close together.

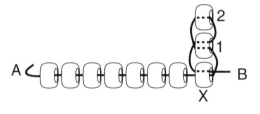

STEP 5
Repeat steps 2, 3
and 4 on side **A**.

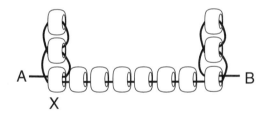

STEP 6
Add two beads to
side **B** and thread side
A through both in the
opposite direction.
Pull tight, the bead will
form a circle to cre-
ate the head.

Continue the body
using the instruction
from the boy on page
42, Step 5.

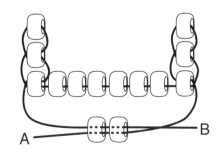

Baby

"Sweet Pea"

STEP 1

Place eight beads on side **B** of your string.
Match the two ends of the string together
and let the beads fall in the middle.

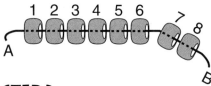

STEP 2

Thread side **A** of your string
through beads number #8-7.

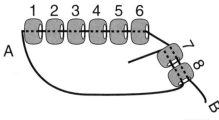

Body stitch,
Leg stitch

▦ **Colors** ▦	
Pink	(31)
White	(9)
String	3 ft.

46

STEP 3

Pull tight to form the head. Make sure the beads are on the center of your string.

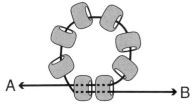

STEP 4

Make the arms by placing 5 beads on side **B**. Skipping beads #5-4-3 thread side **B** back through #2 and #1. Repeat on side **A**.

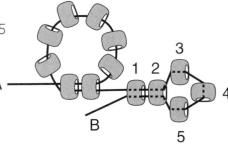

STEP 5

Follow the pattern using the "body stitch" until you reach the legs. Legs are similar to arms. Place 5 beads on side **B**. Skipping #5 and #4 thread side **B** through beads #3-2-1. Repeat on side **A**.

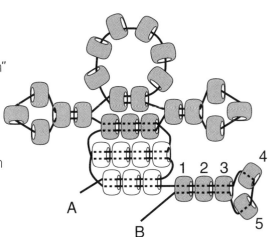

STEP 6

Finish by adding on the last row. Place 2 beads on side **B** of your string. Thread side **A** through both beads in the opposite direction. Tie at the bottom.

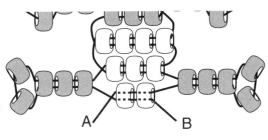

Beaver

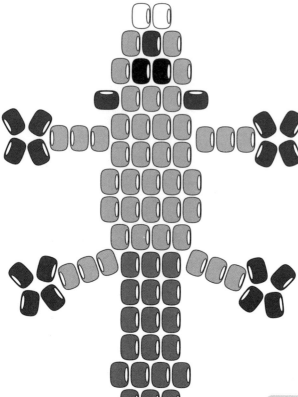

"BUCKY"

Factoid:

The beaver is the builder of the animal kingdom. Gnawing down trees with his sharp front teeth, he builds dams in streams and island lodges to keep the family safe and warm.

Body stitch,
Leg stitch

STEP 1

Start the beaver just like the gecko, using the "body stitch.

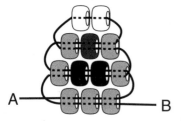

A ———————— B

██ Colors ██	
Black	(2)
Dk. Brown	(19)
Lt. Brown	(21)
Tan	(41)
White	(2)
▬▬ String	5 ft.

48

STEP 2

To make the ears, add one bead to side **B** of your string.

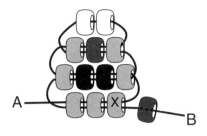

STEP 3

Thread the end of side **B** through the bead marked X and pull tight. Repeat steps 2 & 3 on side **A**.

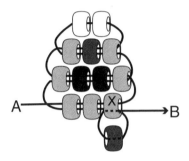

STEP 4

Referring to the pattern add one more row of beads to your animal. To make the legs, place 7 beads on side **B** of your string.

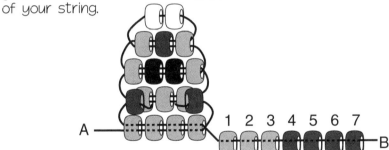

STEP 5

Skipping beads #7-6-5-4, thread side **B** back through beads 3-2-1. Pull tight. If the leg is too far away from the body, hold bead #5 with two fingers and pull the end of string **B**. To finish the beaver, continue the pattern using the body and leg stitch.

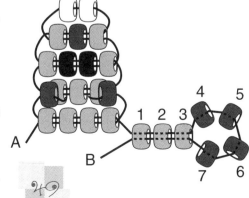

49

Grizzly Bear

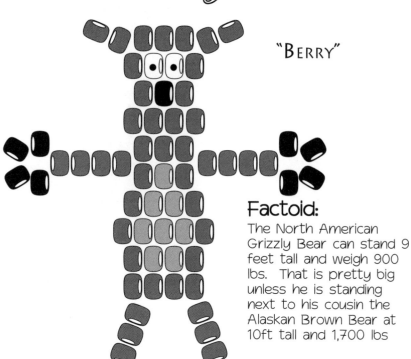

"BERRY"

Factoid:

The North American Grizzly Bear can stand 9 feet tall and weigh 900 lbs. That is pretty big unless he is standing next to his cousin the Alaskan Brown Bear at 10ft tall and 1,700 lbs

Body stitch,
Leg stitch

STEP 1

Place 7 beads on your string. Match the ends and let the beads fall to the center.

A —------ 1 2 3 4 5 6 7 ------ B

▦ Colors ▦

	Color	Count
▮	Black	(17)
▮	Dk. Brown	(46)
▯	Tan	(8)
▢	White	(2)
▬	String	6 ft.

STEP 2

Skipping bead #1, thread side A of your string through bead #2. Skipping bead #7, thread side B of your string through bead #6.

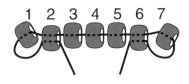

STEP 3

Body Stitch: Following the pattern, place 4 beads on side B of your string.

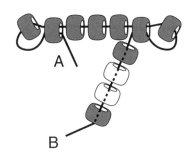

STEP 4

Thread side A through all 4 beads in the opposite direction. Continue following the pattern repeating steps 3 & 4.

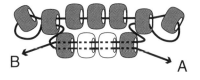

"You can make eyes using a black felt tip marker. Just make a dot on the white beads"

STEP 5

Leg Stitch: To create the leg, place 8 beads on side B of your string. Skipping beads #8-7-6-5, thread side B through beads #4-3-2-1. Pull tight.

Use the skills in steps 1-5 to finish your bear.

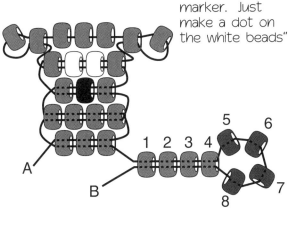

Factoid:

Puppies do not open their eyes until they are more than a week old. They become full grown at 24 months and are considered seniors at 12 years old.

"TRUMAN"

STEP 1

We will start your puppy at the tongue. Place two beads on your string. Match the two ends of the string together so that the beads fall to the center.

A————B

STEP 2

Following the pattern, place 2 beads on side **B** of your string.

A————
B

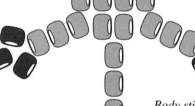

Body stitch, Ear stitch, Leg stitch, Tail stitch

:: **Colors** ::	
Dk. Blue	(13)
Pink	(4)
Blue	(67)
White	(2)
String	6 ft.

STEP 3

Thread side **A** through both beads and pull tight

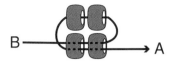

STEP 4

Following the pattern, place 3 beads on side **B** of your string. Thread side **A** through all three beads the opposite way and pull tight. Repeat this step until you reach the ears.

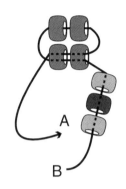

STEP 5

Ear Stitch: To create the ears, place 6 beads on side of your string.

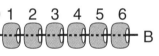

STEP 6

Skipping beads #6-5, thread side **B** through beads #3-4, then through #1-2. Move all beads close to the head before pulling tight.

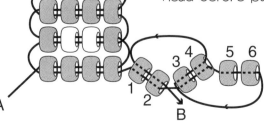

STEP 7

Attach the ear to the head by threading side **B** through the bead marked X. Repeat steps 5-7 on side **A** of your string.

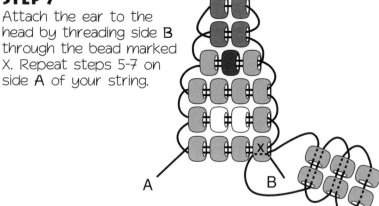

STEP 8

Continue following the pattern using the body stitch until your reach the leg. To make the leg, place 6 beads on side **B** of your string.

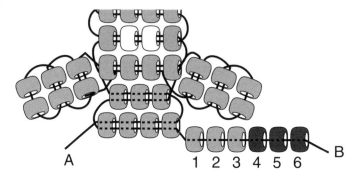

STEP 9

Skipping beads #6-5-4 thread side **B** of your string through beads #3-2-1

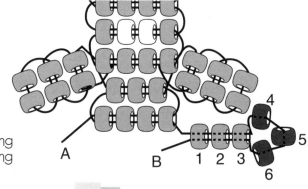

STEP 10

Continue following the pattern using the previous steps

Weiner Dog

"WILLY"

STEP 1
Body Stitch: Build the head until you reach the ears.

STEP 2
To make the ears, place 3 beads on side **B** of your string.

1 2 3

Factoid:
The dachshund was bred in Germany to hunt badgers and other tunneling animals. Dachshund literally means "badger hunter" in the German language

Body stitch, Leg stitch, Tail Stitch

⁙ Colors ⁙

⬤	Purple	(3)
⬤	Brown	(77)
⬤	Black	(16)
▬	String	5 ft.

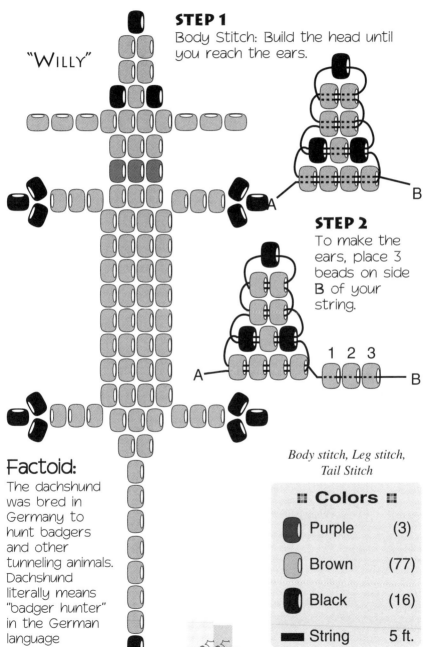

STEP 3

Skipping bead #3, thread side **B** back through beads 2-1 and pull tight. If the ear is too far from the head, hold bead #3 with two fingers and pull the end of string **B**. Repeat steps 2 & 3 using side **A**.

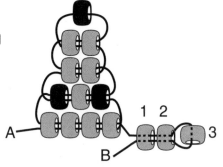

STEP 4

Connect the ears to the head by threading your string through the last bead on each side of the head.

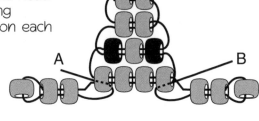

STEP 5

Make the neck using the body stitch in other projects. Place 3 beads on side **B**. Thread string **A** the opposite direction and pull tight. Following the pattern, make 3 rows of 3 beads each.

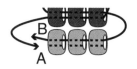

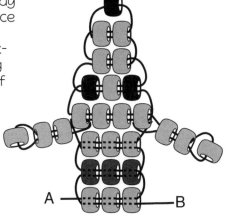

STEP 6

Leg Stitch: Place 6 beads on side **B** of your string. Skipping beads #6-5-4 and thread side **B** through beads #3-2-1 and pull tight.

To make the leg move close to the body, hold bead #5 with two fingers and pull string **B**. Make the other leg using steps 6 & 7.

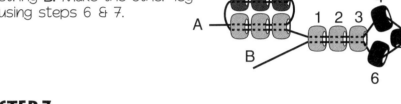

STEP 7

Continue building the remainder of your dog using the body stitch and the leg stitch. The tail is made using the body stitch 1 bead at a time.

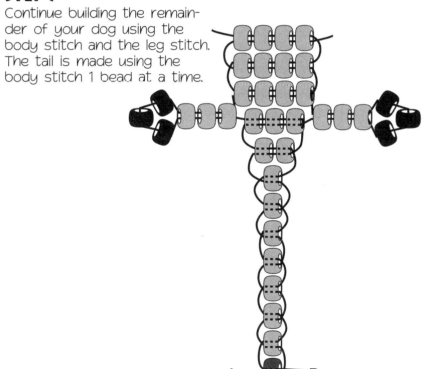

Flower Power

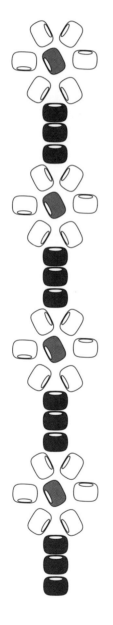

STEP 1

Place 5 beads on side **B** of your string,

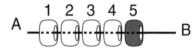

STEP 2

Paying close attention to the direction of the string, thread the end of your string through bead #1.

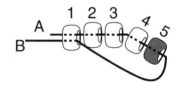

Flower power can be any length. Just keep adding flowers until it is the desired length.

:: Colors ::

●	Green	(12)
●	Yellow	(4)
○	White	(24)
▬	String	3 ft.

STEP 3
Pull tight.

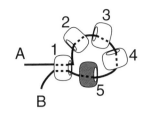

STEP 4
Add two more beads to side **B** of your string.

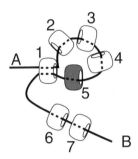

STEP 5
Thread side **B** through bead #4 and pull tight

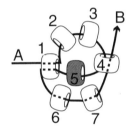

STEP 6
Add 3 separator beads and repeat steps 2 through 6.

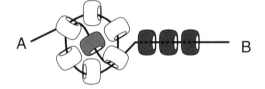

STEP 7
Make as many flowers as required. If you use elastic cording, ends can be tied together and slipped on wrist.

Four Leaf Clover

Factoid:

The Shamrock is a common name for the clover family. Clover normally has three leaves. Some believe that finding a clover with four leaves will bring good luck.

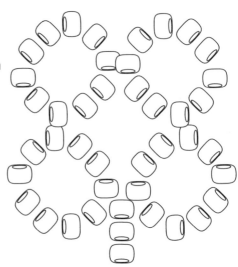

STEP 1

Place 10 green beads on your string.

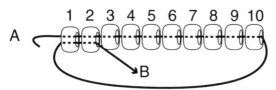

STEP 2

Thread side **B** through bead #1-2. This will form a circle.

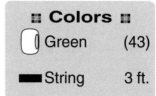

:: Colors ::		
◻ Green		(43)
▬ String		3 ft.

STEP 3

Move the circle down near the end of the string so that side **A** has about 8 inches of string.

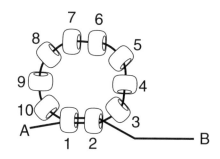

STEP 4

Place 10 green beads on side **B** of your string.

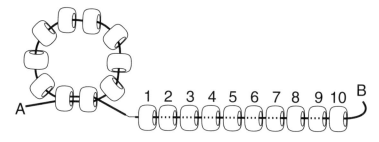

STEP 5

Thread side **B** through beads #1 and #2 and pull tight

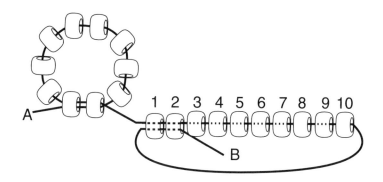

STEP 6

Repeat steps 4 & 5 to form the other leaves. To finish, thread both ends of your string through 3 beads and tie.

Starfish

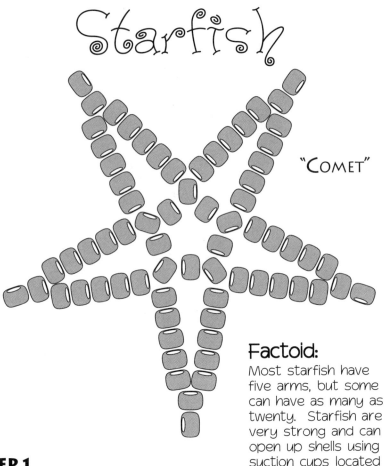

"COMET"

Factoid:
Most starfish have five arms, but some can have as many as twenty. Starfish are very strong and can open up shells using suction cups located on each arm

STEP 1
Place 10 beads on your string.

A —[beads]— B

STEP 2
Tie the string together so that the beads form a circle.
Leave 6 inches of string on side **A**, leave side **B** long.

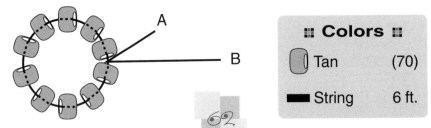

A

B

:: Colors ::	
Tan	(70)
String	6 ft.

62

STEP 3

Place 7 beads on side **B** of your string

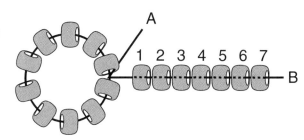

STEP 4

Skipping bead #7, thread side **B** through bead #6. Pull tight.

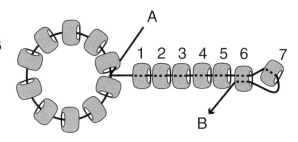

STEP 5

Add 5 more beads to side **B**.

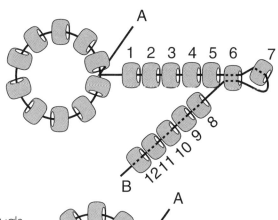

STEP 6

Thread side **B** through the bead marked X on your circle of beads. Repeat steps 2 thru 6 using every other bead on your circle. Tie the ends of your string together after finishing your starfish.

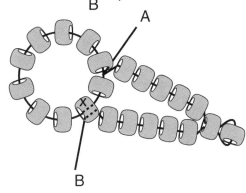

Squid

Factoid:

Squids can rapidly change color to keep hidden on the sea floor. When attacked, they squirt a cloud of black ink in the water and disappear. Although most squid are less than one foot long, some reach fifty feet.

"LENNY"

STEP 1

Start your squid at the top. Place 1 bead on your string. Match the ends and let the bead fall to the middle.

STEP 2

Place 2 beads on side **B** of your string.

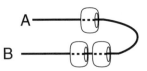

Body stitch,
Leg stitch

▦ Colors ▦

■	Black	(2)
▯	Glow in dark	(156)
▬	String	9 ft.

STEP 3

Thread side **A** through both beads and pull tight.

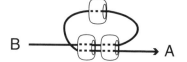

STEP 4

Continue following the pattern using the body stitch until you reach the tentacles.

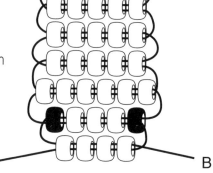

STEP 5

Place 15 beads on side **B** of your string. Skipping the last bead, thread side **B** back through all of the beads. To move the tentacle closer to the body, hold the last bead pull tight. Repeat step 5 on side **A**.

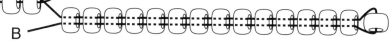

STEP 6

Following the pattern, make a body stitch between each pair of tentacles. Knot after the pattern is complete.

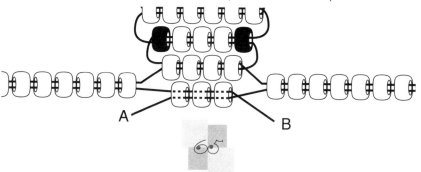

Elephant

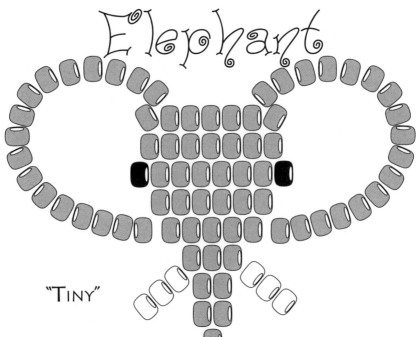

"TINY"

STEP 1

Start the elephant from the trunk using the tail stitch.

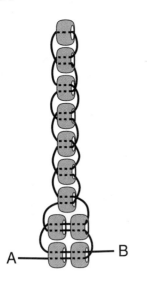

Factoid:

Elephants are the largest land mammals on earth. Their tusks are actually big teeth that stick way out. Elephants have 5 toes on each of their front legs and 3-4 toes on each hind leg.

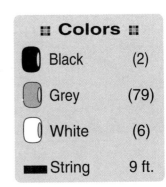

▮ **Colors** ▮	
▮ Black	(2)
▯ Grey	(79)
▯ White	(6)
▬▬ String	9 ft.

STEP 2

Create the tusks by placing 3 white beads on side **B** of your string.

STEP 3

Skipping bead #3, thread side **B** back through beads #2,1. If the tusk is too far from the trunk, hold bead #3 with two fingers and pull your string until it tightens.

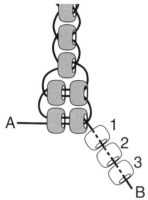

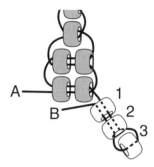

STEP 4

Following the pattern, continue the head using the body stitch. (Basic Body Stitch-Page 8)

STEP 5

Before making the last row on the head, place 1 bead on side **A** and 1 bead on side **B**. Finish the last row using the body stitch.

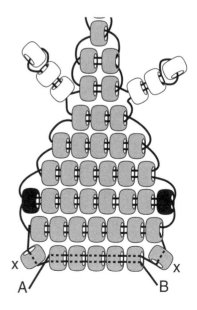

STEP 6

To make the ears, place 17 beads on side **B** of your string.

1 2 3 4 5 6 7 8 9 10 11 12 13 14 15 16 17

B

STEP 7

Thread the end of side **B** through the beads located two rows above the tusks. Repeat steps 6 & 7 on side **A**. Tie the ends together.

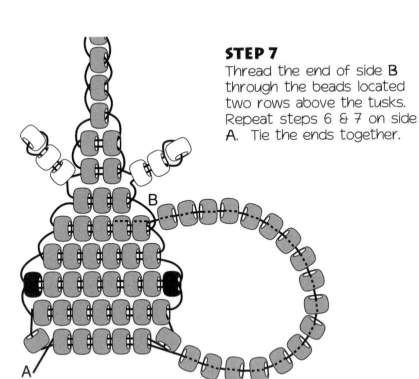

Design Your Own
Bead Animal

69

DESIGN SHEET

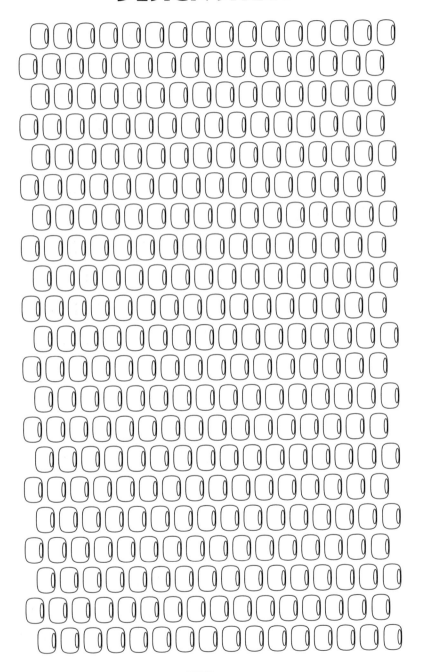

East Enders
Coronation St   Sue Pete
Big Brother   -city
Grange Hill   Derby
Top Gear
The Weakest Link
Ready Steady Cook

71

If you would like to order additional copies of this book
or related products, contact us at:

Bead Man Press
1420 NW Gilman Blvd.
Box 2702
Issaquah, WA 98027

For more convenient ordering call us at (425) 392-3628

or visit our website: **www.thebeadman.com**